FRAME YOUR OWN FUTURE

The Ultimate Guide To Teen Entrepreneurship

MJ TRAPP

TO:_____

FROM:_____

Copyright © 2019 by MJ Trapp

All rights reserved. This book or any portion thereof may not be reproduced or used in any manner whatsoever without the express written permission of the publisher except for the use of brief quotations in a book review.

Edited by: Tiffany Poole

Book Design/Layout: Kantis Simmons

THE SIMAKAN GROUP

Printed in the United States of America

ISBN 978-0-9976581-0-1

Library of Congress Control Number: 2018913381

www.MJTrapp.com

DEDICATION

This book is dedicated to my mother, Mrs. Millie Walker, who brought me into this world.

To my daughter Nicholle who has been my biggest cheerleader and always said, "Mom, you can do it!"

To my family and close friends who were right there pushing me in my back and at least one of them threatened me to get it done or else!

And last, but assuredly not least, to my beloved friend AJ who was my constant encourager, supporter and friend to the end. He took this journey with me.

Thank you all. I finally did it!!!

Table of Contents

Introduction		Page 14
Chapter 1	**See It**	Page 24
Chapter 2	**Write It**	Page 36
Chapter 3	**Plan It**	Page 50
Chapter 4	**Brand It**	Page 64
Chapter 5	**Review It**	Page 72
Chapter 6	**Do It**	Page 82
Chapter 7	**Wrap It**	Page 92
Resources By Chapter		Page 108
More Resources		Page 112
Bibliography		Page 115
Index		Page 121

FOREWORD

Where would I be today without entrepreneurship? That's the question I've asked myself over the last few decades. But I'm thankful for parents, for friends, for mentors, and for books.

If you've ever heard my story, you know that I've spent more than 25 years in school. Yes!

After I was born, I spent my first 6 weeks with my m o m and then I was immediately shipped off to Young World, the nursery where I was raised. I spent 5 years in Pre-K, 7 years in elementary school, 5 years in high school, 4 years in college and then 4 more years in grad school - 25 years.

That formal education opened opportunities for me to work as a Research Scientist at a few amazing companies, including Mobile Chemical Company, NASA's Langley Research Center, and CIBA Vision.

Corporately I was fit, but honestly, entrepreneurship started with me decades ago. My first job was as a landscape engineer: I cut grass.

At the age of eight, I was held responsible for mowing the lawn at the front entrance of my neighborhood. Because of that, and the growth of that business, I had to take on a partner, my best friend JJ. We went throughout the neighborhood cutting the yards of families for $40.00 apiece. That landscape engineering business, aka "I cut grass", ending up growing for the next 10 years, and then I passed the business on to my brother. I went off to college, that same entrepreneurship spirit was still on me.

When I moved to Norfolk State University in Norfolk, VA, I began to cut hair. For $5 a head in my dorm room, I cut hair! I got so good at cutting hair that I had to put a sign-up sheet on my dorm door so that individuals could sign up to have their hair cut by me.

One of the greatest marketing strategies for that "barbershop" in my dorm room is that I put names on that list myself, fake names, to demonstrate that I was busy. That was my first marketing technique for growing my barber business.

Also, while there at college, I had a niche market for ties and bow ties. I went throughout the campus with a black briefcase selling ties and bowties to my professors, the husbands of professors, the fathers of the female students, and *anyone* who was interested in purchasing a tie. Today as an entrepreneur, I create speeches, books, and online courses to help people succeed in school and succeed in life.

Now I ask myself, what if I had MJ Trapp's book at the age of eight? Yes, I had my father, and yes, I had experience, and I even had my ups and downs, but I didn't know at that young age I could *frame my own future*.

Today teens, tweens, and even young adults can frame their own futures by simply reading MJ's book. This book is a step-by-step plan to take your idea to the marketplace. It is a step-by-step plan for what you need to do first, second, and third as a young entrepreneur.

I have a lot of respect for MJ because she's a military veteran in this business, a career woman, and she works to help other veterans. Her passion, her clarity, and her conciseness will help any individual frame his or her future. I encourage you to read this book from the beginning to the end and then read it again and again. Allow *Frame Your Own Future* to be your "go to" book for teen entrepreneurship. *Frame Your Own Future* is the one place you can go to create whatever it is you want in the future.

If I had read this book as a child, perhaps my future, which is now my present would look different. Learn from MJ's examples and create your own future now!

Kantis A. Simmons
Nationally Renowned Motivational Speaker
Best Selling Author of **"Playing Your A Game"**

INTRODUCTION

• • • • • • • • • • • • • •

> "You're off to Great Places! Today is your day! Your mountain is waiting, So... get on your way!" ~ Dr. Seuss[1]

There are so many images and sounds out there to crowd out your thoughts and sometimes it's difficult to figure out what you really want to do. As a child, you may be told what to do and even what to think!

Have you ever considered that finding a solution to a problem could make or save you money? Well, many times the answer is right at your fingertips. In today's age of technology, we literally have access to anything we can possibly imagine. If you think about something long enough and put those investigative skills to work, who knows what you will come up with!

The important takeaway is that you can live your dream and become who you were created to be;

that is unless you are dreaming of becoming a robot! The good news is, you don't have to wait until you're an adult to start your own business, create something uniquely yours, or write blogs or books! Why not?

I can help you manifest your dreams and assist you in making them a reality. This book will show you how: **to write a mission statement, create a simple business plan,** and it will explain in detail **how to get started with your business**. I will also provide you with information about things you may not have considered before starting a business.

Entrepreneurship Defined

Do you want to become an Entrepreneur? You may or may not have ever heard the word or know what an "entrepreneur" is. According to an online source at businessdictionary.com, an Entrepreneur[2] is a person who takes a chance with starting a new business to make a profit.

There are basically two types of entrepreneurs: one who creates a business *for profit* in order to make money and the other is called a Social Entrepreneur[3] who creates solutions for social change without making a profit. Social Entrepreneurs care about solving problems - many times on a large scale. They look at the world around them or some of the big concerns, such as childhood hunger, homelessness, illiteracy, and hatred. Social Entrepreneurs use technology and media to get the support they need to tackle these big problems!

How Young is Too Young?

This book is targeted to Generation Z[4] (Gen Z), those who were born in the early to mid-1990s through 2010.

- Gen Zs are tech savvy.
- Social media has connected them globally to their peers. The internet has connected them globally to knowledge.

Don't think you are ever too young to start a business. There are so many youth entrepreneurs doing what they love, and nobody is stopping them! Go online and see just how many children, (under 10 years old!), and teens are starting a business with little or no money. Many have become very successful. You are not too young to get started, and the time is NOW!

No matter how young you are, your dreams and ideas are valuable. If people have told you that you can't succeed, or that you have no chance in life, don't believe them! If you think you can or if you think you *can't*, you are right either way. This is a paraphrased quote by Henry Ford[5], the guy who invented the Ford automobile. He failed and went broke five times before he succeeded!

If You Think You Can, You Can!

Reading this book will hopefully help you to tap into your creativity, develop those dreams you may already have, or give you some you don't have! I will leave you with tons of resources, websites, and help to motivate and stir up the ideas that I know you already possess. Remember this: **no one** except you can stop what you can do and **no one** except you can talk you out of what you know is deep down inside of you. I will show you many examples of children and teens who have succeeded at accomplishing **great** things because they tried, and they did not give up.

As I said earlier, many inventions and ideas resulted from discovering a solution to a problem. Here's a question for you. What's bugging you? What is *it* that seems so obvious to you that no one else can see? What would you change if you had the opportunity? Okay, now you have the opportunity. So, change *it*!

You could be the next inventor, creator of a game or program, a problem solver, playwright (a person who writes plays), poet, publisher, business consultant, or the next president of your own company or the United States! You could even be the person to find a cure for cancer, AIDS, or some other incurable disease or have the solution for this country's debt problem. The sky is the limit, and you are only limited by your imagination.

Let's face it, when you are young, the one thing that you have is imagination and plenty of it! Why not take those ideas and turn it into money that you can put in the bank! Of course, not everyone is interested in making money to solve a problem. You can create a name, a brand[6], and a legacy that will last longer than you. You also will feel good about yourself and what you can accomplish. This book is for the fast learners and for those who may have thought they would never make it. Well, here's your chance to prove *"them"* all wrong!

For all the children out there, (all ages included), who thought you were some weird little annoying kid or a boring "Brainiac" let's see who will have the last laugh! Now, *you* can laugh out loud! Really.

Chapter Recap

1. This book will show you how to write a

_____

_____

2. A Social Entrepreneur creates solutions for

_____

_____

3. What's bugging you?

_____

Conclusion

I hope you are excited about what lies ahead for you. You can be whatever you choose to be, but *you* must see it first. This book is a personal journey of self-discovery. You cannot and should not allow anyone to talk you out of or steal *your* dream - because it is yours. Dream out loud! What you do with your dream will determine where you go. Your quest begins NOW. Are you ready??? See it, believe it and become it!!!

CHAPTER 1

SEE IT

• • • • • • • • • • • • •

> "Without leaps of imagination or dreaming, we lose the excitement of possibilities. Dreaming, after all, is a form of planning." — Gloria Steinem[7]

There was a time when kids dreamed of things bigger than themselves. Some saw themselves as politicians or high-powered lawyers. As a teen, I dreamed of becoming a radio personality or famous speaker in front of thousands of people! My teachers and other adults often complimented me on my public speaking skills and encouraged me to pursue an education and a career in public speaking. I could actually *see* myself doing it! My life, however, took a different path, but years later I am very close to fulfilling my dream. Remember this, a vision of your success paints a picture of your success. Dream big and keep seeing it!

• • • • • • • • • • • • • •
You cannot bring your dream into reality until you see yourself doing it!

Just as I saw myself as a teen doing things related to public speaking, you can also see yourself doing what you see in your dreams. Hit the bull's eye! In this chapter we will concentrate on steps to identify what you are dreaming, how to focus on your dream and discuss your next steps in bringing your dreams into reality.

An Entrepreneur Who Realized His Dream

Philo Farnsworth[8] invented the first television. It began with a dream of "trapping light in an empty jar." By the time he was 21, he produced the first electronic television transmission. Imagine the things that you can discover about other successful teen entrepreneurs by just surfing the net. Some of those things can "net" you a large bank account or earn you instant fame - if you like that sort of thing.

The good news is you don't have to be a genius to be successful. You simply need to be you.

Can You See It?

What or who pushes *your* button? What makes you leap out of bed in the morning, (please don't say breakfast), or stay up late when you are supposed to be in bed??? In other words, what are you obsessing about or thinking about all the time? Whatever that *thing* is, try to fine-tune it so that you can see it.

When you looked at the picture, what did you see? Did you see a man playing a horn or woman's face? Sometimes you have to take a second look. Can you *see* your idea as a business? Now **focus**. You must see it in your mind first.

What are you dreaming about? Are you dreaming in black and white or in living color? What do you think about most of the time? Reading this book is, hopefully, the beginning of discovering your hidden gift, or your talent, and ultimately *your* business. High achievers and child prodigies are expected to succeed but what about the average everyday B, C, or even D student? At best, if you are lucky, you may end up in a two - year or four - year college and land an average job making average money. Do you believe that's the best life has to offer you? Is that what *you* want?

Perhaps the real problem is, you have not found what excites or interests you - yet.

I am confident that if you are in that forgotten group of average students, you *can* be one of our future leaders, inventors, teachers, writers, poets, politicians, or business owners of not tomorrow, but today! However, it is important to give you the tools you need now to help you become whatever you choose to become. <u>You</u> get to decide your future and you can begin now.

Not convinced yet? Here is another teen entrepreneur who may help to convince you. At the age of 17, Robert Heft[9] had a history project. His project was to redesign the American flag to include Alaska and Hawaii. He constructed a new flag from an old 48-star flag and with $2.87 worth of blue cloth and white iron-on material. Initially, he earned a B minus for his creativity. His grade was later changed to an A after his rendition of the flag was adopted by President Dwight D. Eisenhower!

Streaming Thoughts Exercise

Now it's your turn to see what you can do and become. I want you to try a little exercise to clear your head. Read the statements below a couple of times before actually doing it. If you like, you can play some nice soft elevator music in the background.

1. Close your eyes and take a couple of deep breaths. Seriously, just relax.

2. Let your body go limp and *relax all your muscles*.

3. Think about **one** thing, such as an idea that has been bugging you that you just can't seem to let go. It may be a game, or it may be a song in your head, or a poem. It might even be an invention! Whatever *it* is, see it in your mind and hold on to it. Now open your eyes and write down what you saw.

4. Use the blank space below, your phone notes, or use a sheet of paper to write out your thoughts.

5. It doesn't matter if what you write makes sense right now; just write the things you saw in your mind. Don't worry about grammar or misspelled words at this point. Keep on writing until all your thoughts are finished.

You may need to go through the exercise a few times to complete the process.

Don't try to do anything with what you wrote just yet. You are still in the creation and discovery process, and this could take a little time before it is complete.

Whatever you are seeing, feeling, or sensing - just go with the flow. We will call it "streaming thoughts." Streaming is just writing whatever comes into your head.

The important thing is to understand there is no right or wrong way to do this. These are your ideas and your thoughts. Flow with the process, and you may even start to get excited about seeing your ideas on paper in front of you! Go with that excitement. It may stir up even more things that you thought you had forgotten.

Now tell me, did that writing exercise make you feel powerful - like you are in charge of your future? Do you want to know what to do with the ideas that you just wrote down? Read on. There's more to be discovered.

Chapter 1 Recap

1. Dreaming is a form of _____

_____

_____

2. What does "streaming" mean to you?

_____

_____

3. Robert Heft redesigned

_____

_____

Conclusion

Seeing your dream and writing it down are the first steps toward making your dream come true. It really isn't as far-fetched or difficult as you may have believed. Perhaps you don't know any children or teens who are entrepreneurs. So what? Don't let it stop you from seeing your dreams become a reality.

Most successful entrepreneurs understand that a vision of your success paints a picture of your success! You must see it first!

CHAPTER 2

WRITE IT

• • • • • • • • • • • • • •

"Entrepreneurs don't ask for permission. They act per a mission." ~ Ryan Lilly[10]

When teams are in the creative process and trying to think of ideas about how to do something or come up with a good plan, they sit around a table and brainstorm.

Brainstorming is the process by which one or more people, like a team, try to come up with the best solution to a problem. Before they come up with the best idea, they write down many others to test them out. The team may use a white board, chalk board, or pencil and paper; but they write until the best solution is found.

So, it's the same with your streaming thoughts. You focused on your ideas and started to write the first thing that came into your head. Right? Well, what you wrote down were your streaming thoughts. Streaming is one way of capturing random or "loose" ideas.

Did you enjoy that exercise?

One use for the exercise is to create a mission or vision statement. There is more than one way to write a mission or vision statement. The key is knowing what you want or how you see your company in the future. Once you've determined your mission and vision for the future, you can write your business plan.

Mission Statement Q&A

Mission and **vision** statements are sometimes used interchangeably, although they are different. A company's mission statement describes its purpose and answers the question as to why it exists. It should say who your company is, what you do, what you stand for, and why you do it.

A vision statement provides a description of what the business will look like in the future.

The mission statement is needed when you write your business plan, which will be covered later in the book. Let's focus on what your mission statement looks like from your streaming thoughts. Later, I can talk you through how to come up with a business name. You think you can't do that? Think again. Don't close this book yet! You will thank me later. I *promise* you.

Practice Makes Perfect!

Ok, ready to get started? Here's an example: (Please *don't try to use it* because someone else already thought of it). Let's say you are a neat freak or a little obsessive compulsive. You have an idea of creating a school locker organizer system to get rid of all the clutter and junk most kids have in their school lockers.

In the streaming exercise when your eyes were closed, you may have visualized school lockers with stuff falling out when opened such as books, paper, pictures, shelves, a bulletin board and a small clock. You wrote down everything you saw in the streaming exercise. Hold on to those images for now; we will come back to them.

You may have had ideas about designing a portable school locker organizer, but you never thought of it as a business. At the age of eight, Leanna Archer[11] started her own hair care company, Hair, Inc. She often received compliments on how beautiful and healthy her hair looked and decided to market it! Now she is a business owner. Check out her story: http://www.leannasessentials.com/.

Mission Statement Examples

Now, let's think about ways that you may be able to solve a problem.

Look at those images again that you saw during your streaming exercise: lockers, clutter, stacked books, pictures, disorganization, shelves, a bulletin board, and a clock. Now, let's create a mission statement that answers the question about why your business would exist. Is this starting to make sense to you at all?

Here are some examples of what your mission statement could say:

- *"My company's purpose is to use custom removable shelves so <u>any</u> school locker can be organized within minutes."*

    OR

- *"Our theme is green. Using recycled parts, we save the universe and create organization."*

OR

"Clean and green" portable school locker systems can go anywhere!

Those are simple examples of mission statements created from your streaming thoughts from Chapter One. Use the space provided below to practice some mission statements of your own.

_____

_____
_____
_____

Before you develop your business plan, you need to come up with a name for your business that is uniquely yours and something that fits your business.

What's in a Name?

A name is everything! For example, your name has meaning. If you don't know the meaning of your name, I encourage you to ask your parents or look it up. You may be pleasantly or unpleasantly surprised. Therefore, it's very important to think carefully about your business name. You don't just want it to get attention, you want it to mean something!

Is there a name in your head that describes your business? It may be cute or catchy. You must be careful to make sure your business name is not already in use by someone else. Believe it or not, the things we think of as our creation may have been thought of by others also. Who knew???

• • • • • • • • • • • • •

Once you have a business name in mind, use the website below to verify whether the name is already in use by someone else. http://www.northwestregisteredagent.com/secretary-of-state.html

• • • • • • • • • • • • •

Select the state you reside in and click on "name search." If you put all or a part of a business name in the block, it will bring up the business name if one exists. If the name that you thought of comes up, you can spell it in a different way. Here are some examples.

- For Cars - use "Karz." Using a "z" will give you an "s" sound.

- For "Your" use "Ur" instead. By the way, "ur" is in the Urban Dictionary.

- For joining two words use "n" like "Caps n' Gowns". You can also use a symbol like "&" to join two words.

You can also go to the Small Business Administration for additional tips on choosing a business name.

Chapter 2 Recap

1. _____ is the process by which one or more people, like a team, try to come up with the best solution to a problem.

2. _____ and

_____ statements are sometimes used interchangeably although they are different.

3. _____ started her own hair care company, Hair, Inc.

Conclusion

The primary purpose for having a business plan is for funding, (money), purposes. Having a Mission Statement and a Business Plan means people will take you seriously as a business owner no matter how young you are.

If you need money to get your business idea off the ground or to grow your existing business, a lender, (someone who will invest in your business), will expect, at the very least, that you have a unique business name, a mission statement, and a simple business plan.

Why should anyone invest in your idea if they don't know what it is or how *you* see the business in the future?

A good reason to have a mission statement is that it helps you to focus on why your business exists. The next important step is to create a business plan. We will discuss steps to do that in the next chapter.

CHAPTER 3

• • • • • • • • • • • • • •

"Planning is bringing the future into the present so that you can do something about it now."

~ Alan Lakein[12]

It isn't enough just to want something. You've got to ask yourself, 'What am I going to do to get the things that I want.' You're going to need a plan.

Your challenge is to bridge the gap which exists between where you are right now and the goals that you want to reach. With a definite, step by step plan, you cannot fail, because each step will carry you along to the next step, like a track.

All you need is the plan, the road map, and the courage to press on to your destination. Knowing where you're going is all you need to get there. You can't get lost on a straight road. Author Unknown

When you first get started, you may have a small home-based business operating out of your basement, bedroom, or garage. But as your business grows and you start seeing a profit (money in the bank), you will likely want to move it to a separate space. You need a plan!

In this chapter, you will learn how to write a simple business plan. I will also provide a great example and a template for you to follow.

What's Your Plan?

"You were born to win, but to be a winner, you must plan to win, prepare to win and expect to win." Zig Ziglar[13]

So far, you've "*seen*" your business in your mind during the streaming exercise and written your mission statement. Now it is time to take your idea to the next level.

One of the most important steps to getting someone to take an interest in your idea is to have a plan or a strategy for your business. We call it a business plan. A business plan shows that you have given your idea thought and you have measured its success so that others, (like bankers or investors), can buy into it. Let's revisit the example we used earlier: the portable locker organizer.

More likely than not, you have already tested your idea on yourself and maybe a few friends. You undoubtedly have a useful idea that you can now form a mission statement around. One of our sample mission statements was, **"Using custom removable shelves, *any* locker can be organized within minutes."** Your business plan will describe *how* your mission statement can come into existence. Your plan can be simple or complex, but who wants complex? It all depends on you. For the sake of this example, let's try a simple business plan.

Even a "simple" business plan should contain essential or necessary parts, such as, Executive Summary, Market Analysis, Strategy and Implementation, Organization and Management Team, and Financial Plan and Projections.

Check out this outline for a simple business plan designed for youth entrepreneurs that I got online at Emily Oak's website: http://strongluv.com/business-ideas-kids/.

The Small Business Administration (SBA) is also a great resource for helping entrepreneurs of all ages create a business plan. Remember, your business plan is a changing document, and it will probably change many times to fit your needs.

Your initial business plan may be very short but still contains all the required elements. Here is an example of a method using a template that I created for the portable locker business idea.

Try This One

I. Description of Business

The custom locker storage system is portable and removable. The unit is designed to fit the average school locker. It can be changed to suit the needs of anyone, no matter how picky. The storage device can be designed to fit books, pictures, a small memo board and a mirror in an organized manner inside of a school locker.

A. Business Name and Short History

The business name is "Loc n' Store." The idea of the business came about because of seeing messy lockers and wanting to fix the problem. I designed a storage system that can fit into any school locker and it can go with you at the end of the school year.

B. Describe Your Product or Service

The product is a custom, portable storage locker system. It is flexible interchangeable, made of bamboo, a sustainable and green material, and is bendable. The shelves are made of non-breakable Plexiglas.

C. Location of Business

It is a home-based business located in the basement.

D. Why is this good location?

It is an excellent location because the inventory is small, and supplies can be stored in the basement.

II. Mission Statement:

"Using custom removable shelves, *any* locker can be organized within minutes."

A. Target Market (best customer)

1. My typical customers will be students and faculty.
2. I plan to provide service to at least half of the student body and faculty.
3. My plan is to advertise with flyers and to set up a locker to demo the product.

B. Competition

1. Local hardware stores have similar products, but they cost more.
2. On-line stores also have similar products, but I can meet the demand easier and faster.

III. Market Strategy

A. Sales Strategy

1. I will sell the locker storage system for $15 apiece.
2. I have already sold $5,000 in products online.

3. It costs $5.00 to produce one unit and materials are readily available at local hardware stores.

B. Inventory

I will maintain an adequate inventory of supplies based on the original pre-orders for the product and future sales projections.

IV. Management/Personnel

A. Employees

1. At the start-up phase of the business, there will be no employees. However, after the initial phase, there may be one to three employees.
2. As the owner and CEO, any employees that I hire will be Sales Associates assisting with sales.

B. Payroll
1. Each Associate will earn $2.00 for each unit sold.

2. When an Associate sells 25 or more units, the Associate will earn $2.50 for each unit sold.

If someone else is funding your business, they will have lots of questions about their investment that may be answered best in a simple, but well-written and well-prepared business plan. It will all make sense to you later, I assure you.

At this point, I don't want you to get stuck on having to have a business plan to operate your business. Hopefully, there is someone that you can trust who will be willing to help you when you're ready. Do not give up on your dream after coming so far in the process.

Picture yourself successful and able to meet all your financial needs.

For more information, in addition to the websites mentioned, please talk to your business teacher if you have one, guidance counselor, business owners in the community, or ask your parents for guidance. You would be amazed how much parents can help you.

Chapter 3 Recap

1. One of the most important steps to getting someone to take an interest in your idea is to have a _____ _____.

2. A business plan should contain _____ or_____parts.

3. You would be amazed how much _____ can help you.

Conclusion

You do not have to use everything in the outline to get your plan off the ground. Your business plan *will change* as your business grows and changes. Having a business plan is an important step in establishing the credibility of your business. It will give you that edge over other businesses who may not have done their homework. The reason is simply that you have a plan or a road map to help you get where you desire to go. Sometimes we overlook the obvious. Stick to the plan, and you will reach your goal.

To be taken seriously, you must do your homework! Show someone your business idea that you trust and who wants you to succeed. As you've seen in the examples in previous chapters, other children and young adults have started successful businesses. Why not you? Start with a plan, do the work, and expect success!

CHAPTER 4

BRAND IT

> "If you're not branding yourself, you can be sure others do it for you."
>
> Unknown

In today's world it is so easy to get caught up in the hype! Everywhere you look, there are images. Images can speak volumes. There is an old saying, "a picture is worth a thousand words," and I get that! When you think about a brand, what is the first thing that pops into your head? No doubt, you may think about clothing/ product labels, record labels, thousands of commercials we see on television, or colorful billboards that we pass every single day. What about actors, entertainers, various industries, or even politicians? Could ALL these things possibly fall into the category of brands? When we finish the discussion in this chapter about brands, I know you will have a clearer understanding of what a brand is.

Brand Defined

Simply put, your brand is your identity. It is how people perceive you both personally and professionally. Did you know you can express your brand as a name or symbol? Jay Baer[14] said it this way, "Branding is the art of aligning what you want people to think about your company with what people actually do think about your company. And vice-versa." In other words, you are your brand. When people see your name, they see a reflection of honesty, integrity, quality, humor, reliability, caring, and concern - or the complete opposite. As you establish your company, it is important to understand your business represents you and the image people have of you, good or bad. Be careful how you handle yourself and your business.

Brands and Logos

Is there a difference between a brand and a logo? They are not the same, exactly. A logo can be known as a brand mark or a brand icon. It is also a graphic symbol that represents a person or organization.

I'm sure that a few prominent companies come to mind in the beverage industry, sports apparel, or even eyewear! When you see their logo, you have a visual experience or memory of that experience, good or bad. There are companies that were well respected at one time that are no longer thought of in that light because of current negative biases. Your integrity is everything! Remember to honor your word in your businesses and success will eventually come. When you put your brand out there, make sure that you can stand up to the scrutiny.

Brand Identity and Marketing Your Business

Now that you know a bit more about branding, how will it help to grow your business? That's a good question! Let's explore more about your brand identity beginning with a definition. "Brand identity is the message the consumer receives from the product, person, or thing and it will connect product recognition."- Laura Lake[15]

For consumers, (people who buy your products), to receive the message that you intend for them to receive, you must be intentional. In the business plan, we discussed target marketing, which is identifying and determining what it takes to reach your desired customers. For example, if your business is writing short stories about monsters, what will you do to identity the best way to reach people who love to read short stories about monsters? You may do surveys at a library, send emails to everyone you know who reads, and place flyers in places people who like to read may visit.

Of course, you could also use social media to get it all done faster! If you continue to stick with the process, results will come. Your audience, or those who buy your products or services will receive your message loud and clear.

Chapter 4 Recap

1. Your brand is your_____.

2. Remember to honor _____ in your businesses.

3. _____ is the message the consumer receives from the product, person, or thing and it will connect product recognition.

Conclusion

The subject of branding is an important one for you to understand as an entrepreneur.

The most important aspects of your brand are integrity, honesty, and consistency. Be the person that you represent. When people see, or hear your name, or see your logo, the message they receive will hopefully be a good one. This chapter is not all-inclusive, and I do not want to go on and on about the subject of branding. Explore the topic more on your own if you need more information. Feel free to reach out to your business teachers, school libraries, or local businesses to gain better insight on this topic. Start thinking about what this means to you and how you will express your brand!

CHAPTER 5

REVIEW IT

• • • • • • • • • • • • • •

> "Twice and thrice over, as they say, good is to repeat and review what is good." ~ Plato[16]

Have you ever turned in work in a hurry and wish you had taken five extra minutes to look over it? When we don't give something that second look or review, we miss the obvious. How frustrating that is! There's nothing worse than receiving a B or a C when you should have received an A. Why didn't you take that second look?

In business, we can also miss the obvious. Reviewing the information, you acquired in the previous chapters is a way to retain what you've learned. You are more likely to recall and apply the principles if you rehearse them. Practice makes perfect!!!

You were introduced to a lot of new information in the previous chapters.

The purpose of this review is to slow down and go over what you previously learned before adding more information.

Review - Redo

Here is where we stop and make sure that we are on point before we move forward. I call this the review process. We will go back to the beginning of the process and re-trace our steps. In this chapter, we will use a workbook format to see how much you remember from what we covered earlier.

What is the exercise we used to allow your ideas and creativity to flow?

_____

_____

_____

In that exercise, what were some of the things that you "saw?"

_____

_____

_____

What is a "Mission Statement" and why is it important to have one?

_____

_____

_____

What is a Vision Statement?

_____

_____

_____

While a Business Plan is not something that you may need to start your business, name three good reasons to have one.

_____

_____

_____

Name three parts of a Business Plan.

_____

_____

_____

What is YOUR reason for wanting to start a business?

_____

_____

_____

Define "brand" in your own words.

_____

_____

_____

What is the difference between *brand* and *logo*?

_____

_____

_____

Your Passion is Your Business

If one of your reasons for starting your business is passion, then you are in good company. Sam Colt[17] had a passion for all things mechanical. He often disassembled and reassembled his father's firearms just to see how they worked. At the age of 16, he attended an academy to study navigation; but because he was mischievous, he was expelled. His father sent him out to sea on a ship for a year so that he could learn navigation firsthand. While on the ship, he became fascinated with the ship's wheel. This fascination resulted in the creation of his first revolver with a six-barrel cylinder, locking pin, and hammer carved out of wood. Amazing!

Conclusion

I firmly believe that the youth of today can be today's business owners, inventors, or social entrepreneurs, in whatever area they choose! Who said you *have to* wait to get to some magic age to become successful? I want you to believe that you can be successful while you are still young. As stated earlier, some businesses require very little or no money to get them up and running. All it takes is your imagination! If you don't have any ideas of your own, check out some of these! https://www.entrepreneur.com/article/159548.

CHAPTER 6

> "Do not wait for someone else to come and speak for you. It's you who can change the world"
>
> ~ Malala Yousafzai[18]

It's your move! Often what we put off doing takes less time than we thought it would. I don't know about you, but there are things I wish I had done sooner. A great example is writing this book. I started writing this book more than five years ago, but I got stuck. Life happened! I encourage you to move forward with your business idea no matter how difficult it may become. Just keep it moving! I will give you all the resources to succeed that I wish I had five years ago. With the resources I provide in this chapter, you can get your business off the ground and become a legal business owner! The steps are not difficult to follow; I try to keep it simple.

You can always expand if you like. Your idea to start your business is not limited to a brick and mortar building. It can be virtual or even an "app". Many businesses in recent years have been started without a physical location. Twelve-year-old teen pastry chef, Ashalah Michelle Wright[19] created two businesses called, Cook Me Up A Notch and The Kid Chef Dreams Academy (https://www.cookmeupanotch.com/about).

This celebrity teen chef is a business owner, philanthropist, and writer! Check out her cookbook, *"City of Dreams"* in bookstores.

What is your idea that you may have buried because no one is doing it – yet? There is always a first. Why not you?

Summing it Up

Here are the practical steps to legally set up your business.

1. Register Your Business Name:

To legally operate your business in the state in which you reside, you must register it. The following website will give you contact information for all the Secretary of State Offices in the nation (http://www.northwestregisteredagent.com/secretary-of-state.html). You can also reach out by phone and ask questions if needed when you are ready to register your business. Business name registration is commonly known as making a "Doing Business As" (DBA) filing. DBA filings are also known as "assumed name" or "fictitious name" registrations. A business registers a DBA name when the name of the business is something other than the business owner's legal name.

2. Apply for a Business License:

A Business License, Occupational License, or Home Occupation Permit is a government certificate that most starting businesses must get whether the business is: a retail business, a home - based business, e-commerce, or online. Check http://www.sba.com/georgia/licenses-permits/ under business resources by the state to make sure you are following the laws of the state in which you live.

3. Apply for a Tax Identification Number:

Why do you even need a Tax Identification Number or Employer Identification Number (EIN)? As a business owner, you must file taxes. All the money that you make from your business is taxable unless you operate as a Not for Profit organization. That's another story and another book!

According to the IRS website, your EIN is your *permanent number* and can be used immediately for most of your business needs, including opening a bank account or applying for business licenses.

Go to: https://www.irs.gov/ or https://www.irs.gov/ businesses/small-businesses-self-employed/ to apply-for-an-Employer-Identification-Number-(EIN)- online.

4. Open a Business Bank Account:

It is strongly advisable to open a business account at your bank or credit union. It keeps your business affairs neat and tidy. You can keep up with your spending as well as what your company makes as it grows. Also, keep all business-related receipts to account for your spending because you will need those receipts when you file taxes at the end of the year. I recommend purchasing a zippered pouch and making a habit of throwing your receipts in there to keep them filed safely away for a later time.

In addition to the four steps above, I also **highly** recommend visiting the US Trademark and Patent Offices (https://www.uspto.gov/) if necessary, and the US Copyright Office (http://www.copyright.gov/). For example, if you want to make sure no one steals your invention, you should patent it. To protect your unique business name, you should trademark it because it gives you and your business the exclusive rights to use the name, brand, or logo in the United States. You can use this link below for the Small Business Administration for additional tips: https://www.sba.gov/starting-business/choose-register-your-business/choose- your-business-name

It is worth your time, effort, and money to visit the sites and watch the videos that pertain to your situation. I also suggest visiting the Trademark Office **before** you register your business name.

Ask me how I know! When I applied for a trademark for Frame Your Own Future® my application was initially suspended because someone with a similar name, in another state, had applied for a trademark before I did. It was months and months of going back and forth with the US Trademark Office before I was able to prove our businesses were *dissimilar* enough to approve both applications.

Sometimes, it's worth the fight. In my case, it was a win-win!

Chapter 6 Recap

1. Many businesses in recent years have been started without a _____ _____.

2. According to the IRS, your EIN is your

_____

3. If you want to make sure no one steals your invention, you should _____ it.

Conclusion

I have given you many things to consider and to take in small, bite-size pieces. I do not want you to get lost in the processes; however, they are necessary for you to become successful business owners. My goal is to give you just enough information to get your business off the ground, but not too much to confuse you. In the last and final chapter, I will give you my parting thoughts and even *more* resources.

CHAPTER 7

WRAP IT

• • • • • • • • • • • • • •

"It is the 'follow through' that makes the great difference between ultimate success and failure, because it is so easy to stop." ~ Charles Kettering[20]

It's a wrap! We're at the end, but it is the beginning for you. This is the last chapter and the last business advice I have for you. My goal at the onset was to inspire you to follow your dreams or to get one if you don't already have one. I provided examples and took you through all the steps necessary to help you accomplish your goals. It is now up to you.

Why reinvent the wheel, so to speak? You can model a success story, for inspiration, that resembles your idea but make it your own.

This book is filled with wonderful examples of children and teens who have accomplished phenomenal success. They started, followed through, and achieved success. Your success doesn't have to look like anyone else's. Just be *your* best self.

Here is where you take what you gleaned from this book and put it into practice. It's up to you now. You will never be alone on this journey. Knowledge is at your fingertips!

More Motivation

I have provided you with enough resources to get you off the ground and beyond. Whether your idea is an invention that needs a patent or written material that needs to be copyrighted - you know where to go to find everything that you need. You also have information on how to register your business name, (for your protection), and how to apply for a business license. I tried to think of all the things that you would need to get you started.

The rest is up to you. What I can't do for you is to get you off the sofa or the video game. While you are playing it, please consider that you *could* create a better one – just maybe. Or if not a super video game, perhaps an app. Maybe you write great song lyrics, and you know the lyrics are good! Get the lyrics out of your head and on paper. And *please* don't give your lyrics away! Follow the steps to get them copyrighted with *US Copyright* and *Library of Congress*.

What if you have an idea that can revolutionize the world the way the invention of computers did? What if *your* idea can make you a millionaire overnight? It is possible, but as I have said and continued to say, you must believe it.

Teen Business Organizations

There are some other groups I have not mentioned which could be helpful to your business.

One of these is Junior Achievement (JA): https://www.juniorachievement.org/web/ja-usa/home.

I urge you to go to the website and check it out. They have programs beginning in elementary school! Junior Achievement is an excellent organization that is sure to boost your confidence and creativity if you get involved. As a teen, I joined JA, and it impacted me greatly. Real business leaders volunteer to mentor young teens and teach them the "how" and "why" sides of business. They show you sound business principles. Part of that process is, in fact, starting your own "junior" business. As a student, you take on various roles in the business, such as owner, Chief Executive Officer (CEO), and Chief Financial Officer (CFO). It was interesting, and I had great fun learning all about business.

Some schools have an organization called Future Business Leaders of America (FBLA) http://www.fbla-pbl.org/.

If your school has one, it may be beneficial to get involved. Another resource is your school guidance counselor or career advisor.

I realize that not all schools have caring counselors, but some do. It's worthwhile to give them a chance. I have heard from students that some counselors do not take an interest in them nor do they encourage "average" students, let alone under-average students. Try approaching your guidance counselor with a believable idea - one you have already researched. He or she may be more willing to take you seriously and guide you in the right direction. It's worth a try.

Whatever route you choose to pursue, get assistance with starting your business. Remember this, do not allow to anyone to put out your fire. If your first idea isn't great, so what?! Keep dreaming and streaming. You will eventually come up with an idea that will work. *"Only those who dare to fail greatly can achieve greatly."* Robert F. Kennedy[21]

Successful People Who Failed

There are many people who will encourage you and become your personal cheering squad if you let them. Whatever your circumstances may be, you can make it - with or without the support of anybody else. Believe in yourself first and watch things happen!

There are many talented and successful teen entrepreneurs that you can find on any search engine or social media site. I believe that reading their stories will give you that extra boost to do what you were created to do! If they did it, why can't you?

Here is one that might inspire you. Thomas Edison's 22 teachers said he was "too stupid to learn anything." He was fired from his first two jobs for being "non-productive." As an inventor, Edison made 1,000 unsuccessful attempts at inventing the light bulb. When a reporter asked, "How did it feel to fail 1,000 times?"

Edison replied, "I didn't fail 1,000 times. The lightbulb was an invention with 1,000 steps."

"Our greatest glory is not in never falling but in rising every time we fall." ~ Confucius[23]

MJ's Last Words

As you begin this exciting journey of your life, I will put myself in your shoes when I was a teen. I can speak to some of your concerns:

- **You are not alone**. There are thousands of teens and kids already in business and many are quite successful! Reach out to them and who knows, one of them will probably be willing to share some tips with you.

- **Connect with other teen entrepreneurs or kidpreneurs through social media.** There are many social media groups out there but please use caution before getting involved with any group. Check them out first (please) to make sure they're legit. Bring a trusted adult with you to any meeting (even a virtual meeting).
- **Learn from the mistakes of others.** Whatever your idea is, no matter how good it is, it may be an idea someone else has already tried.
- **It's probably going to cost you more time, money, and effort than you thought it would.** Make up your mind before you start to be committed to the end, at whatever the cost.

- **Prepare to be discouraged or talked out of your business idea.** Sometimes the people closest to you will offer the least support! Don't allow anyone to throw rain on your parade. You can do this!

- **Trust your gut.** In the process of getting your business going, if someone wants to invest, and it sounds too good to be true, it could be! Talk you your parents or another adult that you really trust before agreeing to sign **anything**!

Chapter 7 Recap

1. Learn from the _____ of others.

2. As an inventor, Edison made _____ unsuccessful attempts at inventing the light bulb.

3. It is the _____ _____ that makes the great difference between ultimate success and failure.

Conclusion

I could go on and on with advice and examples of famous people who failed before they succeeded, but *they* succeeded!

If the individuals mentioned in this book *eventually* succeeded because they did not give up, you can too. You can do whatever you choose to if you try. The ball is in your court. It's your turn to succeed!!! I look forward to seeing you out there doing business!

NOTES

RESOURCES BY CHAPTER

See It

Philo Farnsworth
https://www.biography.com/people/philo-t-farnsworth-40273

Robert Heft
https://www.reference.com/history/created-50-star-american-flag-b313b519c345f7b

Write It

Leanna's Hair

http://www.leannasessentials.com/

Plan It

Business Plan Template
file:///C:/Users/mjtra/Downloads/kid-business-plan-worksheet.pdf

Review it

Teen Business Ideas
https://www.entrepreneur.com/article/159548

Do It

Ashalah Michelle Wright
https://www.cookmeupanotch.com/about

Register Your Business Name
http://www.northwestregisteredagent.com/secretary-of-state.html

https://www.sba.gov/starting-business/choose-register-your-business/register-your-business-name

Apply for a Business License
http://www.sba.com/georgia/licenses-permits/

Apply for a Tax Identification Number
https://www.irs.gov/businesses/small-businesses-self-employed/apply-for-an-employer-identification-number-ein-online?_ga=1.262204236.1387624645.1480371367

Patent and Trademark Offices
https://www.uspto.gov/

US Copyright Office
http://www.copyright.gov/

Wrap It

Junior Achievement
https://www.juniorachievement.org/web/ja-usa/home

FBLA
http://www.fbla-pbl.org/

People who failed on their first attempt
http://www.budbilanich.com/50-famous-people-who-failed-at-their-first-attempt-at-career-success/

MORE RESOURCES

Young Inventors
http://www.younginventors.org/

Idea Finder
http://www.ideafinder.com/features/classact / young.htm

Teen Inc. Magazine
http://www.teenink.com/About/

Young Poet Society
www.youngpoetssociety.com

Kids Business
http://www.moneyinstructor.com/art/childbusiness.asp

Teaching Kids Business
http://www.teachingkidsbusiness.com/ business-plan-program.htm

Kids Online Business School
www.onlinebusinesscoach.com/business- school-for-kids

Create Your Own Invention
http://printables.familyeducation.com/inventions/printable/4752.html

Young Entrepreneurs Alliance
http://www.g20yea.com/

Fee Schedule for Patents and Trademarks
https://www.uspto.gov/learning-and-resources/ fees-and-payment/uspto-fee-schedule

18 Under 18: Meet the Young Innovators Who Are Changing the World
http://fortune.com/2016/09/15/18-entrepreneurs-under-18-teen-business/

Bibliography

1. "A Quote from Oh, The Places You'll Go!" *Goodreads*. N.p., n.d. Web. 20 Apr. 2017.

2. "Entrepreneur- Read the full definition." *BusinessDictionary.com*. N.p., n.d. Web. 20 Jan. 2017.

3. Root. "Social Entrepreneur." *Investopedia*. N.p., 26 Oct. 2010. Web. 20 Jan. 2017.

4. Williams, Alex. "Move Over, Millennials, Here Comes Generation Z." *The New York Times*. The New York Times, 18 Sept. 2015. Web. 20 Apr. 2017.

5. "Henry Ford Quotes (Author of My Life and Work)." *Henry Ford Quotes (Author of My Life and Work)*. N.p., n.d. Web. 19 Jan. 2017.

6. "What Is Brand? - Definition from WhatIs.com." *WhatIs.com*. N.p., n.d. Web. 21 Apr. 2017.

7. Gloria Steinem, George Barris (Photographer), and Gloria Steinem Ruchira Gupta (Editor). "Gloria Steinem." *Goodreads*. N.p., n.d. Web. 21 Apr. 2017.

8. "Philo T. Farnsworth." *Biography.com*, A&E Networks Television, 17 May 2016, www.biography.com/people/philo-t-farnsworth-40273.

9. Heft, Robert. "Who Created the 50-Star American Flag?" *Reference*, IAC Publishing, www.reference.com/history/created-50-star-american-flag-b313b519c345f7b.

10. "Entrepreneurs Don't Ask for Permission. They Act per a Mission. Ryan Lilly." *Best Quotes Ever*. N.p., n.d. Web. 21 Apr. 2017.

11. "Leanna's Essentials - All Natural Products." Leanna's Essentials - All Natural Products. N.p., n.d. Web. 19 Jan. 2017.

12. "Alan Lakein Quotes." *BrainyQuote*, Xplore, www.brainyquote.com/quotes/alan_lakein_154655.

13. "Zig Ziglar Quotes - BrainyQuote." N.p., n.d. Web. 19 Jan. 2017.

14. "Branding 101: Brand vs. BRANDING." *J. Genow Marketing*, 17 May 2018, jgenowmarketing.com/brand-vs-branding/.

15. Lake, Laura. "Learn How Brand Identity Is Defined and the Role It Plays in Marketing." *The Balance Small Business*, The Balance Small Business, www.thebalancesmb.com/brand-identity-and-marketing-2295442, Web. 17 May 2018.

16. Flowloop. "Twice and Thrice Over, as They Say, Good Is It to Repeat and Review What Is G... - Plato at Lifehack Quotes." *Quote by Plato*. N.p., n.d. Web. 21 Apr. 2017.

17. History.com Staff. "Samuel Colt." *History.com*, A&E Television Networks, 2009, www.history.com/topics/inventions/samuel- colt.

18. "Do Not Wait for Someone Else to Come and Speak for You. It's You Who Can Change the World - Malala Yousafzai." *Women for One*. N.p., n.d. Web. 21 Apr. 2017.

19. "Cook Me Up A Notch | Atlanta Teen Bakery." Cook Me Up A Notch | Celebrity Teen Baker, Web. 17 May 2018.

20. "Charles Kettering Quote." *A-Z Quotes*. N.p.,n.d. Web. 21 Apr. 2017.

21. "Robert F. Kennedy Quotes." *BrainyQuote*. Xplore, n.d. Web. 21 Apr. 2017.

22. "Job Search." *Bud Bilanich*, budbilanich.com/50- famous-people-who-failed-at-their-first-attempt-at-career-success/. Web. 17 May 2018.

23. "Confucius Quotes." *BrainyQuote*. Xplore, n.d. Web. 21 Apr. 2017.

Index

A

Average	28,29,55,97

B

Brainiac	21
Brand	20,65,66,67,77,78
Brand Identity	68
Branding	65,66,68,69,70
Bull's eye	26
Business name	39,43,44,45,46,55,85,88,94
Business plan	16,38,39,43,46,47,52,53,54 59,61,68,76,77

D

Doing Business As (DBA)	85
Dream	15,16,18,19,22,25,26,28,33 34,59,84,93,97

E

EIN (Employee Identification Number)	86,87,89
Entrepreneur	10,11,16,17,18,26,29,34 37,54,69,79,98,100

F

Focus	26,28,37,39,47	
Frame Your Own Future	11,89	
Future Business Leaders of America	96	

G

Generation Z   17

J

Junior Achievement (JA)   96

K

Kidpreneurs   100

L

Library of Congress   2,95

Logo   67,70,78,88

M

Mission statement   16,38,39,41,42,46,47,52,53 56,75

P

Philanthropist   84

R

	Review	6,73,74
S		
	Secretary of State Offices	85
	Small Business Administration (SBA)	45,54,88
	Social Entrepreneur	17,21,79
	Social media	17,69,98,100
	Solution	15,17,19,20,21,37,45
	Streaming	31,33,37,39,40,41,42,52,97
T		
	Target marketing	57,68
	Tax Identification Number	86
	Teen entrepreneurs	11,26,29,98,100
U		
	US Copyright	88,95
	US Trademark and Patent Offices	88,89
V		
	Vision	25,26,34,38,76

Vision Statement 38, 76

Y

Youth Entrepreneurs 18, 54

CPSIA information can be obtained
at www.ICGtesting.com
Printed in the USA
LVHW050823301222
736050LV00009B/1129